NEW ENGLAND
4 Seasons of Wonder

Michael J. McCormack

Schiffer Publishing Ltd

4880 Lower Valley Road • Atglen, PA 19310

Other Schiffer Books by the Author:
Timeless Crossings: Vermont's Covered Bridges.
ISBN: 978-0-7643-3830-4. $34.99

Other Schiffer Books on Related Subjects:
Along Route 7: A Journey Through Western New England.
Stephen G. Donaldson.
ISBN: 978-0-7643-3372-9. $45.00
New England's Natural Wonders: An Explorer's Guide. John S. Burk.
ISBN: 978-0-7643-3983-7. $34.99

Designed by Justin Watkinson
Type set in Bernhard Modern BT/Arrus BT

ISBN: 978-0-7643-4441-1
Printed in China

Published by Schiffer Publishing, Ltd.
4880 Lower Valley Road
Atglen, PA 19310
Phone: (610) 593-1777; Fax: (610) 593-2002
E-mail: Info@schifferbooks.com

For the largest selection of fine reference books on this and related subjects, please visit our website at **www.schifferbooks.com.** You may also write for a free catalog.

This book may be purchased from the publisher.
Please try your bookstore first.

We are always looking for people to write books on new and related subjects. If you have an idea for a book, please contact us at proposals@schifferbooks.com

Schiffer Books are available at special discounts for bulk purchases for sales promotions or premiums. Special editions, including personalized covers, corporate imprints, and excerpts can be created in large quantities for special needs. For more information contact the publisher.

In Europe, Schiffer books are distributed by
Bushwood Books
6 Marksbury Ave.
Kew Gardens
Surrey TW9 4JF England
Phone: 44 (0) 20 8392 8585; Fax: 44 (0) 20 8392 9876
E-mail: info@bushwoodbooks.co.uk
Website: www.bushwoodbooks.co.uk

To my mother for her gift of imagination,
and my father for his gift of determination—
this book is dedicated with love to you both.

Acknowledgments

I wish to sincerely thank the following individuals for their friendship, support, and patience during the many years I've struggled to bring my life's work to a wider audience: Kathleen Egan, the late Tracey Egan, Marc Ferland, Jay Guidone, John McCormack, Josh, Lynne McCormack, the late Marybeth McCormack-Howard, the late Michael G. McCormack, Robert McCormack, and Jim Scully. My gratitude also to the following organizations: Natural Resources Defense Council, oldschoolphotolab.com, The Poetry Foundation, and Schiffer Publishing.

Contents

Plymouth Notch, Vermont

My introduction to the majesty of New England came at the age of six when I traveled to the "Northeast Kingdom of Vermont" with my family on what would be the first of many summer vacations we would take together. There, along the quiet shores of Lake Willoughby, I discovered a world that had only been hinted at previously during the countless hours I spent running wild with my childhood friends in the small tract of woods that bordered our tiny neighborhood, tucked neatly away within the suburbs of southern Connecticut.

We had arrived at a place where waters of unfathomable depths were surrounded by green mountains of shocking heights—where forests extended like verdant oceans to the horizon, full of clear running icy streams from which you could fish for brook trout that would later find their way to your supper plate. Northeastern Vermont is a land where nighttime skies are so amassed with infinite clusters of stars, that a boy could easily imagine they represented distant cities in the heavens yet to be discovered—and that refuge could be found in the natural world that surrounds us all.

A chord was struck and, although it would be another decade before I would receive a camera of my own as a Christmas gift, without my knowing it, a photographer was born that summer. Subsequent summers sent my parents packing up their station wagon and trekking with their four kids to the beaches of Cape Cod, Connecticut's Lake Quonnipaug, or to New Hampshire's Lake Winnipesaukee and White Mountains. Winters brought us to the Berkshires of western Massachusetts or the Green Mountains of Vermont, where my brothers and I skied all day down trails of freshly groomed snow, and then nearly ate our parents into poverty with appetites fueled by adrenaline and the cold mountain air. As it has for so many millions of others, the New England landscape had become our playground, drawing us again and again toward its aura of possibility and escape.

The past two decades found me roaming that very same landscape, in every conceivable kind of weather, with my camera gear in tow, while I searched for my next photograph. Photography, much like writing, can be a lonely endeavor at times. You rise at ungodly hours, are at the mercy of the notoriously fickle New England weather, and often find yourself in the right place at the wrong time, just as the light dissolves behind an unruly bank of clouds—or the perfect view is suddenly obscured by throngs of tourists. What has kept me here in the northeast pursuing this art is the sense that no matter how many images I may capture, there is always a little bit more of the mystery to be unveiled, and that there is wisdom to be mined from these ancient hills and distant shores that beckon just beyond our reach. My photography has always been an attempt to breach that gap. I am humbled by the task, but proud of the effort. I am a New Englander!

Michael McCormack
Summer 2012

Reading, Vermont

As the last of the glacial ice sheets departed from the North American continent over 10,000 years ago, an evolving 72,000 square mile area east of the Hudson River Valley extending all the way to the Atlantic Ocean's swells was finally unveiled. The earth has since developed many places that combine the drama of grand mountain peaks, serene woodlands, pastoral hillsides, and rugged coastal scenes, but nowhere does this rich amalgam of geography form a more stirring or timeless symphony than in New England.

Always more than the sum of its varied terrain and quirky background, New England, and the six states that constitute it, had its genesis in nature's tumult and has been luring people to its call ever since. As rich in human as it is in natural history, it has been a testing ground for the principles of religious tolerance, liberal democracy, and transcendentalist philosophy. All of which continue to leave their mark on history, for more than any other part of America, New England ties the promise of the country's origins to the restless contradictions of the modern age.

New Englander's are acutely aware of this extraordinary legacy, for here it is as inescapable as the passage of time itself. Yet you are as likely to hear one boast about New England's contributions to the greater good, as you are of seeing the Red Sox move from their beloved Fenway Park. Perhaps Walt Whitman understood the Yankee temperament better than anyone when he wrote "To know us go to our mountain tops and ocean shores." The incomparable vistas one can enjoy along New England's nearly 5800 miles of coastline, or from one of 67 peaks that reach over 4000 feet in elevation, surely have something to do with our expansive view of human nature.

But it is the elements that shape those very same places, which also serve to temper the New Englander's perspective, for to exist here requires a subtle acquiescence to the laws of a climate that on any given day can produce weather as varied or volatile as the northeast's own storied past. The weather in this part of the world has become as deeply imbedded in the fabric of New England's culture as clam chowder, and is almost as savory. It is a land where the temperature can drop to as low as 50 degrees below zero, as it did in the tiny village of Bloomfield, Vermont, during the winter of 1933—or can soar to a sweltering 107 degrees Fahrenheit, as happened in New Bedford, Massachusetts, during the summer of 1975. Yet, to be a true New Englander is to embrace the ephemeral nature of beauty, to know that the blue skies will inevitably bring the clouds, which can only serve to heighten our appreciation of the moment. We are at one with loss, but would have it no other way.

"Nature always wears the colors of the spirit," wrote another favorite New England literary son—Ralph Waldo Emerson, and as each year progresses from spring through the inevitability of winter, the landscape becomes an expressive canvas for the respective joys and wonders that each season brings to it. Walk through Boston's Public Garden in early May amidst the tulips and canopies of cherry blossoms, and feel your senses rise above the sounds of the traffic on Arlington Street to another realm beyond the city. Sit at sunrise along Otter Cove at Maine's Acadia National Park in summer, as the roar of the crashing surf and first rays of light embrace to celebrate the birth of another day. Make your way to Peacham, Vermont, when the autumn leaves are peaking in color, hike along any of the back roads leading away from the center of the village, and you will

Introduction
The Colors of the Spirit

"One of the brightest gems in the New England weather is the dazzling uncertainty of it."

—Mark Twain

find yourself in a world where beauty is the only truth worth knowing. Drive along the Kancamagus Highway of New Hampshire in winter when the White Mountains live up to their name, stop at the overlooks to view the distant ranges, and the sound of the wind whispering through the ancient passes will leave you speechless.

New England's distinctive four-season climate has over time become its single most defining characteristic, challenging New Englander's with its legendary unpredictability, while at the same time rewarding the senses with its eternal display of nature's remarkable capacity for resiliency and sustenance. It is the gift of change that has inspired artists and poets alike with its promise of storm clouds forever looming on the western horizon, but magnificence that is only a sunrise away.

Spring

"Spring—an experience in immortality."

—Henry David Thoreau

Sugar Hill, New Hampshire

The first flush of Spring in New England, and the exuberance of life it brings with it, is a wonder to behold, rivaled only by the full blaze of autumn. The end of shortened days and abrasively cold nights signals nature's most dramatic exhortation of the year. The impoverished landscape once again erupts in a riot of color and long desired scents carried on breezes, which hint of even better days to come.

From the Litchfield Hills of Connecticut to the Great North Woods of New Hampshire, stands of birch, oak, beech, and maple are awash with budding leaves, while streams and waterfalls overflow from snow melt and frequent spring downpours. Short-lived plants like dandelions come to life first, followed by perennials like daffodils, daisies, lupines, and lilacs. Apple orchards are alight with blossoms that cling from branches like suspended snowflakes the winter forgot. Outdoor fairs and festivals line town greens and city parks, bringing New Englander's of all stripes together again to share music, food, or the arts, while the Red Sox commence with another long season in the hopes of bringing one more championship back to Fenway Park.

With the preceding season now a distant memory, the New England spring resonates with one of the region's most deeply held historical convictions—that suffering ultimately brings redemption.

Perkins Cove / Ogunquit, Maine

West Coventry, Rhode Island ◥

◤ Back Bay / Boston, Massachusetts

◣ Londonderry, New Hampshire

Sugar Hill, New Hampshire ▶

◀ Hollis, New Hampshire

Marshall Point Lighthouse / Port Clyde, Maine ◣

◀ Prescott Park / Portsmouth, New Hampshire

15

White Mountains, New Hampshire

Derry, New Hampshire

Stowe, Vermont

Boston Public Garden / Boston, Massachusetts ▷

Boston Public Garden / Boston, Massachusetts ◣

◤ Boston Public Garden / Boston, Massachusetts

Marshall Point Lighthouse / Port Clyde, Maine

Acorn Street / Boston, Massachusetts ◤

◥ Hollis, New Hampshire

Londonderry, New Hampshire ◣

Boston Public Garden / Boston, Massachusetts

Marble House / Newport, Rhode Island ◥

Prescott Park / Portsmouth, New Hampshire ◤

Boston Public Garden / Boston, Massachusetts

◤ Boston Public Garden / Boston, Massachusetts

Drakes Brook / White Mountain National Forest, New Hampshire ▼

◀ Sunderland, Vermont

Portland Head Lighthouse / Cape Elizabeth, Maine

Sugar Hill, New Hampshire ▼

◤ Londonderry, New Hampshire

Boston Public Garden / Boston, Massachusetts ◣

◢ White Mountains / New Hampshire

Londonderry, New Hampshire ▼

◤ Marlborough Street / Boston, Massachusetts

Nauset Beach / Cape Cod / Orleans, Massachusetts ▶

◤ Marshall Point Lighthouse / Port Clyde, Maine

◣ Roseland Cottage / Woodstock, Connecticut

Sunset / Beavertail State Park / Jamestown, Rhode Island

Pomfret, Connecticut ◥

West Arlington, Vermont ◥

◤ Glen Ellis Falls / Jackson, New Hampshire

Prescott Park / Portsmouth, New Hampshire ◢

1923.

Greene, Rhode Island ◢

◣ Portsmouth, New Hampshire

Pomfret, Connecticut ◢

Hancock Tower / Boston, Massachusetts ◢

◣ Trinity Church / Newport, Rhode Island

Warner House / Portsmouth, New Hampshire ◢

Newport, Rhode Island ◢

St. George, Maine

Moss Glen Falls / Granville, Vermont

West Coventry, Rhode Island ◣

◤ Sunderland, Vermont

Sunrise / White Mountains, New Hampshire ◣

◤ Back Bay / Charles River / Boston, Massachusetts

Ogunquit, Maine ▼   ◤ Woodstock, Connecticut

Yawkey Way / Fenway Park / Boston, Massachusetts ◢

Yawkey Way / Fenway Park / Boston, Massachusetts ◤

◤ Hamilton, Massachusetts

Stair Falls / White Mountain National Forest / New Hampshire ▼

◥ Perkins Cove / Ogunquit, Maine

◢ Boston Public Garden / Boston, Massachusetts

Prescott Park / Portsmouth, New Hampshire ◥

◤ Pomfret, Connecticut

Brooklyn, Connecticut ◣

◢ Windsor, Vermont

Glen Ellis Falls / Jackson, New Hampshire ▶

Block Island, Rhode Island ◀

◀ Block Island / Rhode Island

Beebe River Falls / Campton, New Hampshire

Lake Massabesic / Auburn, New Hampshire ▼

Sugar Hill, New Hampshire ◣

◥ Troy, Vermont

55 Mt. Vernon Street / Boston, Massachusetts ▷

Mt. Vernon Street / Boston, Massachusetts ◥

◣ Beacon Hill / Boston, Massachusetts

Marlborough Street / Boston, Massachusetts ▶

▼ Dusk over Back Bay / Charles River / Boston, Massachusetts

◀ Cape Cod Lighthouse / Truro, Massachusetts

Pemaquid Point Lighthouse / Bristol, Maine ▼

Sunrise / Rye, New Hampshire ◣

◥ Stonington, Connecticut

42

Londonderry, New Hampshire ▶

◤ Pomfret, Connecticut

Hollis, New Hampshire ◣

◣ Stair Falls / White Mountain National Forest / New Hampshire

◥ Windsor, Vermont

◢ York, Maine

Woodstock, Vermont ▶

Summer

"Every year, the end of summer,
lazy and golden, invites grief and regret"

—Maxine Kumin

Sunset / Halibut Point / Rockport, Massachusetts

If springtime in New England entices its patrons to once again reclaim the landscape as their own, the birth of summer, with its promise of extended light and warmth, compels New Englander's—from Newport to Stowe—to seek refuge within it. In this region, summer represents the year's coming of age, with all of its lavish hopes finally realized in a place and time where the possibilities for escape are seemingly endless.

Here, summer and its affable climate make it possible to find solitude upon the most distant reaches of the Appalachian Trail, and watch humpback whales breach the ocean's surface from a beach along Cape Cod—all in the same day. A beautiful New England summer day is unlike any other during the year, for each one gently issues a silent imperative which rises above the well known resolute Yankee pragmatism, challenging us with the notion that the distant dreams of youth may still be salvageable, but the moment is not.

Haunting in its radiance—yet poignant in its brevity—summer in New England is a celebration of life, and nature's grandest invitation to live it to the fullest.

Mt. Monadnock summit / Jaffrey, New Hampshire ◤

Mt. Washington summit / Presidential Range / White Mountains, New Hampshire ◤

◣ Appalachian Trail from Mt. Lafayette / Franconia Notch, New Hampshire

Hampton Beach State Park / Hampton, New Hampshire

Scotch Beach / Block Island, Rhode Island

Monhegan Island, Maine

Crane Beach / Ipswich, Massachusetts

Rockport, Massachusetts ◥

◤ Seal Harbor, Maine

Stonington Harbor / Stonington, Connecticut ◥

◤ Sunset / Newport, Rhode Island

North Square / Boston, Massachusetts

Sunset / Herring Cove Beach / Provincetown, Massachusetts

Rockport, Massachusetts

Nubble Lighthouse / York, Maine

Rockport, Massachusetts

Mystic, Connecticut ▶

First Branch of the White River / North Tunbridge, Vermont ◣

◤ Woodstock, Vermont

54

Field Box 59 / Fenway Park / Boston, Massachusetts

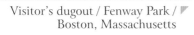

Visitor's dugout / Fenway Park /
Boston, Massachusetts

York, Maine

Burlington, Vermont

Fenway Park / Boston, Massachusetts

Bennington, Vermont

Bennington, Vermont

Fenway Park / Boston, Massachusetts

Stonington, Connecticut

Perkin's Cove / Ogunquit, Maine

West Quoddy Head Lighthouse / Lubec, Maine ▶

◤ Meredith, New Hampshire

◤ The Green Monster / Fenway Park / Boston, Massachusetts

Portsmouth Harbor Lighthouse / New Castle, New Hampshire ◥

Otter Cove / Acadia National Park, Maine

Block Island, Rhode Island ◣

Ipswich Bay / Annisquam, Massachusetts ◿

Gloucester, Massachusetts

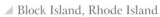
Gloucester, Massachusetts

Sunrise / Rye Harbor, New Hampshire

Block Island, Rhode Island

White Mountains, New Hampshire

Grafton Notch State Park / Newry, Maine

Sugar Hill / White Mountains, New Hampshire

Back Bay / Charles River / Boston, Massachusetts

Pemaquid Point Lighthouse / Bristol, Maine

 Head of the Meadow Beach / Cape Cod / Truro, Massachusetts

Cape Neddick / York Beach, Maine

Herring Cove Beach / Cape Cod / Provincetown, Massachusetts ◢

◣ Gloucester, Massachusetts

Portland Head Lighthouse / Cape Elizabeth, Maine ◢

Cape Cod National Seashore / Truro, Massachusetts ◥

◣ Marconi Beach / Cape Cod / Wellfleet, Massachusetts

Woodstock, Vermont

Bennington, Vermont

Stark, New Hampshire

Bluff's Beach / Block Island, Rhode Island

Cahoon Hollow Beach / Cape Cod / Wellfleet, Massachusetts

Sunset / Annisquam, Massachusetts

Sunset / Newport, Rhode Island ◥

Sunset / Block Island Sound / Rhode Island ◤

◤ New Harbor, Maine

Monhegan Island Lighthouse /
Monhegan Island, Maine

Nauset Beach / Cape Cod / Orleans, Massachusetts

Nauset Lighthouse / Cape Cod /
Eastham, Massachusetts

Nauset Lighthouse / Cape Cod /
Eastham, Massachusetts

Nauset Lighthouse / Cape Cod /
Eastham, Massachusetts

69

Rockport, Massachusetts ▶

◀ Block Island, Rhode Island

Perkin's Cove / Ogunquit, Maine ◣

◀ Rockport, Massachusetts

Portland Head Lighthouse / Cape Elizabeth, Maine

Pemaquid Point Lighthouse / Bristol, Maine

 Marconi Beach / Cape Cod / Wellfleet, Massachusetts

Hampton Beach State Park / Hampton, New Hampshire

Block Island, Rhode Island ◥

The Berkshires / Sheffield, Massachusetts ◥

◣ Glen Ellis River / Jackson, New Hampshire

Sunset / Annisquam Lighthouse/ Annisquam, Massachusetts

Marshall Point Lighthouse / Port Clyde, Maine

Monhegan Island Lighthouse / Monhegan Island, Maine

Nubble Lighthouse / York, Maine

Back Bay / Charles River / Boston, Massachusetts

 Marshall Street / Boston, Massachusetts

North Square / Boston, Massachusetts

Halibut Point / Rockport, Massachusetts ◤

Ballard's Beach / Block Island, Rhode Island ◣

◤ Hampton Beach State Park / Hampton, New Hampshire

Ocean Path / Acadia National Park, Maine

Annisquam Lighthouse / Annisquam, Massachusetts

York Beach, Maine

Sunset / Ipswich Bay / Rockport, Massachusetts

Autumn

"There is no season when such pleasant and sunny spots may be lighted on, and produce so pleasant an effect on the feelings, as now in October"

—Nathaniel Hawthorne

Peacham, Vermont

The New England autumn, emerging in the wake of summer's heat, is one of nature's most accomplished feats of sheer beauty, as well as the coming winter's overture. Enhanced by the chlorophyll-depleting frosty evenings and sun-drenched days, New England's fall foliage spectacle has to be witnessed firsthand to be truly appreciated, for aside from the Tohoku region of Japan, it simply has no equal anyplace else in the world.

With the first crisp days of mid-September, the higher elevations of northern New England become a vivid patchwork of hues, ranging from the soft yellows of birch leaves to the muted purples of the ash, all highlighted by the area's most dazzling tree—the sugar maple. The coming equinox sends the earliest phases of luminous color careening down valleys and spreading across the lower tiers of Maine, New Hampshire, and Vermont. As temperatures continue to drop throughout October, autumn's foliage display makes its fiery run south and crosses the borders of Massachusetts, Connecticut, and Rhode Island.

Autumn is New England's signature season, and its most duplicitous, for it hides beneath its artful veneer the sobering promise of a more unforgiving climate in the months to come. But its temporal state only makes New Englander's treasure it more and bask in its glory long after its luster has faded by December. The falling of leaves and subsequent browning of the earth is a moving elegy to the miracle of existence in a world whose rhythms we increasingly struggle to come to terms with. Despite this, its allure remains as timeless as a first love—its rewards sweeter than apple cider.

New Preston, Connecticut ◣

St. Johnsbury, Vermont ◣

◣ Deering, New Hampshire

Londonderry, New Hampshire ▶

Jordan Brook / Acadia National Park, Maine ▶

84

Danville, Vermont ▶

◀ White Mountain National Forest, New Hampshire

Acadia National Park, Maine ▼

▼ Glen Ellis Falls / Gorham, New Hampshire

85

West Dover, Vermont

Silver Cascade / White Mountains, New Hampshire ▶

◣ Londonderry, New Hampshire

◢ Bethel, Maine

Roxbury, Connecticut ◥

Reading, Vermont ◥

◤ Hinsdale, Massachusetts

Richmond, Rhode Island

Hamilton, Massachusetts

Washington, Connecticut

Ipswich, Massachusetts

White Mountains / Sugar Hill, New Hampshire

Jenne Farm / Reading, Vermont

Peacham, Vermont ▼

◤ Swift River / White Mountains, New Hampshire

◢ Boston Public Garden / Boston, Massachusetts

93

Woodstock, Vermont ▶

Pinkham Notch / White Mountain National Forest, New Hampshire ◥

◤ Gilford, New Hampshire

Derry, New Hampshire ▶

◀ Peacham, Vermont

Richmond, Rhode Island ◣

◢ Center Sandwich, New Hampshire

White Mountains / Sugar Hill, New Hampshire ▶

Reading, Vermont ◣

96

◤ Hamilton, Massachusetts

Stair Falls / White Mountain National Forest, New Hampshire ▼

◤ Newfane, Vermont

◣ Peacham, Vermont

Marlow, New Hampshire ▼

◤ Block Island, Rhode Island

◢ White Mountain National Forest, New Hampshire

Milton, Massachusetts ▶

◥ Peacham, Vermont

◤ Tunbridge, Vermont

Ipswich, Massachusetts ◥

◣ Albany, New Hampshire

◣ East Barnard, Vermont

Meredith, New Hampshire ◤

◥ New Preston, Connecticut

Boston, Massachusetts ◣

◢ Londonderry, New Hampshire

Milton, Massachusetts ▶   ◀ Woodbury, Connecticut

102

Peacham, Vermont

East Barnard, Vermont

Wenham, Massachusetts ▶

◥ New Preston, Connecticut

◢ White Mountain National Forest, New Hampshire

Peacham, Vermont ▶

▼ West Cornwall covered bridge / West Cornwall, Connecticut

Thetford, Vermont ◣

◢ Long Pond / Belvidere, Vermont

Londonderry, New Hampshire ◥

◤ Hamilton, Massachusetts

107

Waitsfield, Vermont ▶

◤ Milford, Connecticut

Bennington, Vermont ▶

◤ Moultonborough, New Hampshire

ROBERT LEE FROST
MAR. 26, 1874 ~ JAN. 29, 1963
"I HAD A LOVER'S QUARREL WITH THE WORLD"
HIS WIFE
...INOR MIRIAM W...
1873 ~ ...

108

Danville, Vermont

Joe English Hill Brook / New Boston, New Hampshire

Hamilton, Massachusetts

112

Hamilton, Massachusetts ◢

◣ Bethel, Maine

Marlboro, Vermont ◤

Ripley Falls / White Mountain National Forest, New Hampshire ◥

◣ Weston, Vermont

◢ Cabot, Vermont

Auburn, New Hampshire ▼

◤ Holderness, New Hampshire

◣ Holderness, New Hampshire

Peacham, Vermont

Amherst, New Hampshire ▶

◤ Tamworth, New Hampshire

New Preston, Connecticut ◣

◤ Randolph, Vermont

Peacham, Vermont ▶

◀ Jordan Pond / Acadia National Park, Maine

117

Lower Aspetuck Falls / New Preston, Connecticut ▶

Pinkham Notch / White Mountains, ▶
New Hampshire

◀ Ledge Brook / White Mountain National Forest,
New Hampshire

Auburn, New Hampshire ▶

◣ St. Johnsbury, Vermont

◣ Coventry, Rhode Island

◣ Hamilton, Massachusetts

Reading, Vermont ▶

◀ Haverhill, New Hampshire

119

Hudson, New Hampshire ▶

◀ Hamilton, Massachusetts

◢ Deering, New Hampshire

Meredith New Hampshire ◥

◤ Pomfret, Vermont

◤ Beaver Brook / Woodstock, New Hampshire

121

Milton, Massachusetts

Winter

"Where the sun shines now no warmer
than the moon."

—Robert Frost

Amherst, New Hampshire

No other season in New England offers such a curious set of challenges and rewards as does the long winter that envelops the northeastern United States in December, in some years refusing to relinquish its icy grip until April's merciful arrival with the spring.

While New Englanders' ingenuity in dealing with the trappings of a frozen environment—from the institution of downhill skiing to the tapping of maple syrup—might be viewed as a sign of character, it is ironically the winter's innate stillness that is most in synch with the region's celebrated traits of restraint and honesty, born out of three centuries' worth of constant battle with the ever changing elements. And despite being a land that remains steeped in lasting historical bonds, here as in most places in the northern hemisphere this time of year, people have come to depend upon the technological prowess of twenty-first century civilization as a means for coping with the relentless cold and reduced daylight. Yet, a snowstorm in New England slackens the pace of modern life by necessity, melding hardship with bliss, creating moments for unanticipated introspection and enlightenment.

Winter's appeal in New England lies in its unique ability to transform even the most mundane tract of land into an implausible dreamscape from which the season is no longer viewed as a test of endurance, but rather, an opportunity for surrender.

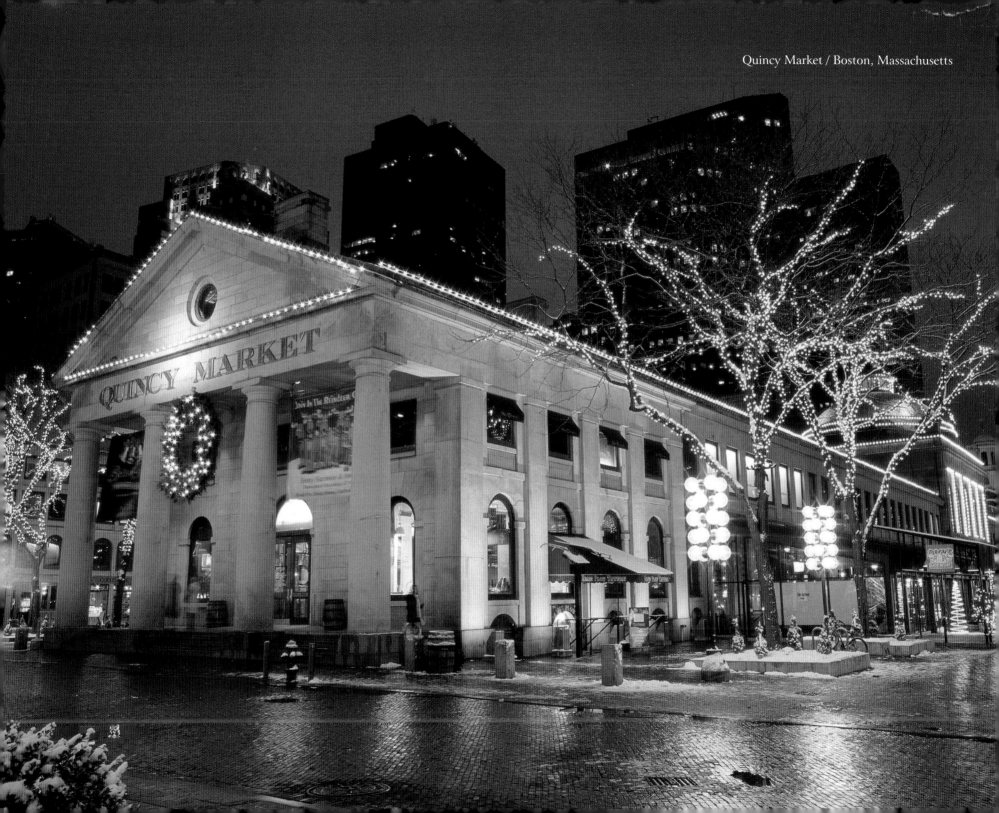

Quincy Market / Boston, Massachusetts

Portland Head Lighthouse / Cape Elizabeth, Maine

White Mountains / Livermore, New Hampshire ◥

◥ Woodstock, Vermont

Pomfret, Vermont ◣

◢ Boston Public Garden / Boston, Massachusetts

Piscataquog River / New Boston, New Hampshire

Weathersfield, Vermont ▶

◥ Lake Massabesic / Auburn, New Hampshire

◣ Newburyport, Massachusetts

Boston Common / Boston, Massachusetts

Marlboro, Vermont ◣

◥ Quincy Market / Boston, Massachusetts

Deering, New Hampshire ◢

Cape Cod National Seashore / Eastham, Massachusetts ▶

◀ Jenne Farm / Reading, Vermont

Boston Common / Boston, Massachusetts ◥

◢ White Mountain National Forest, New Hampshire

York, Maine ▼

◣ Woodstock, Vermont

135

Portsmouth, New Hampshire

138

Quincy Market / Boston, Massachusetts ▼

▼ Portland Head Lighthouse / Cape Elizabeth, Maine

▲ Bedford, New Hampshire

Eastford, Rhode Island ▶

▼ Boston, Massachusetts

▲ Beacon Street / Boston, Massachusetts

139

Deering, New Hampshire ▶

Deering, New Hampshire ◣

◤ Reading, Vermont

Marlboro, Vermont ◤

◤ Amherst, New Hampshire

Quincy Market / Boston, Massachusetts ◥

◤ York, Maine

141

142

Manchester, New Hampshire ▼

◤ Jenne Farm / Reading, Vermont

◣ Boston Public Garden / Boston, Massachusetts

Sugar Hill, New Hampshire ▶

◤ White Mountains, New Hampshire

143

Woodstock, Vermont

Mount Washington / Presidential Range / Bretton Woods, New Hampshire

Deering, New Hampshire ▶

◀ Deering, New Hampshire

Cornwall, Connecticut ◣

◥ Quincy Market / Boston, Massachusetts

Hillsborough, New Hampshire ▶   ◀ Grafton, Vermont

147

York, Maine ▶

◀ Portsmouth, New Hampshire

Eastford, Rhode Island ▶

◀ Portland Head Lighthouse / Cape Elizabeth, Maine

◀ Sugar Hill, New Hampshire

Boston, Massachusetts ▼

Crane Beach / Ipswich, New Hampshire ▼

Tuckerman Ravine / Mount Washington / ▼
White Mountains, New Hampshire

◤ Beacon Hill / Boston, Massachusetts

149

Lake Winnipesaukee / Gilford, New Hampshire ◥

◥ Stowe, Vermont

Piscataquog River / New Boston, New Hampshire ◣

◢ Belknap Mountains / Gilford, New Hampshire

Beacon Street / Boston, Massachusetts

◀ Bethel, Vermont

◀ Arlington Street / Boston, Massachusetts

151

Stowe, Vermont ▼

◤ Bedford, New Hampshire

152

Amherst, New Hampshire ▼

◤ Nubble Lighthouse / York, Maine

◤ Bennington, Vermont

Mount Lafayette / Cannon Mountain / Sugar Hill, New Hampshire ▶

◀ Bedford, New Hampshire

Boston Public Garden / Boston, Massachusetts ▶

◀ Cornwall, Connecticut

153

Nauset Lighthouse / Eastham, Massachusetts ▼

▼ White Mountain National Forest / Lincoln, New Hampshire

▲ Holderness, New Hampshire

Woodstock, Vermont ▼

Woodstock, Vermont ◣

155

◤ Woodstock, Vermont

State House / Boston, Massachusetts ▼

Robert Gould Shaw Memorial / ▼
Boston, Massachusetts

Quincy Market / Boston, Massachusetts ▼

▼ Auburn, New Hampshire

◢ York, Maine

Sugar Hill, New Hampshire ▶

Holderness, New Hampshire ◀

◀ Goshen, Connecticut

158

Rockport, Massachusetts ▶

◀ Rockport, Massachusetts

Hillsborough, New Hampshire ◣

◢ Marlboro, Vermont

159

Bedford, New Hampshire ▶

▼ Strawbery Banke / Portsmouth, New Hampshire

◀ Sunrise / Magnolia, Massachusetts